Writing Our Way Through Life

A Self Coaching Workbook

Christie Victress Close

Table of Contents

"Everything in life wants to move in a creative and prosperous direction. I can align myself with this natural movement and bes provided with everything I need now."

Introduction to Self Coaching

Fourteen years ago I realized that I had not formed any goals because I believed I didn't have choices like other people. After admitting that I needed help, I slowly saved up enough money to hire a success coach. Speaking with him on the phone for an hour every two weeks was a tremendous help. He offered the strong supportive parent voice I needed to hear. Writing helped keep that positive voice with me. I began clinging to every positive thought and began writing my way through major life changes.

I wrote pages about every concern and about all I wanted but dared not hope to have or do in my future and about feelings and unmet needs. I wrote about my past and present then slowly approached writing about the future. Changes came by relying on my coach and transforming obsolete beliefs through experimental writing and actions. During the next two years I succeeded in changing my career and financial circumstances dramatically. All the while I was increasing my self-esteem and ability to choose and achieve goals consciously. I learned how to help myself stay with the process when it got challenging and find my way around problems by reading my workbook and writing in it again. I discovered it was essential to celebrate each step and approach life with more curiosity.

The purpose of this self-coaching workbook is for you to develop your own inner coach and mentor who will always be with you as a unique, personal and creative resource. Some of us work through life challenges best at our own pace in total privacy and with no approving or disapproving feedback. If this is your preference, then you will enjoy using this workbook. It contains my favorite personal growth skills and creative writing processes. These have been simplified to include just the essential information for you to use with ease.

I recommend that you write in your own handwriting, rather than on a computer. Writing by hand facilitates a connection to the feeling and dreaming side of ourselves with access to a relaxed, meditative state most would find hard to achieve at a keyboard. There is only a small amount of reading to do in this process. It is my hope that what I have included here will inspire you to write often, to rewrite and toss out many pages while you find your own way. I have chosen recycled paper because you will no doubt use plenty of paper while refining your writing until it is crystal clear and precise.

I sincerely hope this workbook becomes your coach, and your solace in times of stress. As often as possible read the most powerful messages you have written to remind yourself of your strengths and goals. Then write about the future changes you desire and design them. This writing process can clarify your vision and help you discover your way-finding ability.

This is a "just-do-it" approach. When using this method you do not need to know how to accomplish your goals. Instead you will brainstorm freely, write lists of actions and do them with curiosity. The way that works for you will be revealed as you go forward. Writing Our Way, W.O.W. supports you because it is so precisely designed for you in exactly the way no one else could provide. Empowering yourself by completing an important goal will build your self-worth and esteem far beyond previous limits.

Each year this practice will become more satisfying. Just think how amazing it will be to look back on ten years of celebration. Thank you for embarking on this journey and as you "just-do-it" energetically, remember to balance with rest and celebrate often.

"The purpose of this self-coaching workbook is for you to develop your own inner coach and mentor who will always be with you as a unique, personal and creative resource."

Organizing Your Work Book

The idea of providing you with a binder rather than a book came from my own experience. When I began making my "goals binder" it was just a place to keep a journal that I wrote to express my struggles and to help me deal with the blues. It evolved into this organized form. One thing I discovered about the workbook is that as I took care to keep it current and clear of clutter, it also took care of me.

The workbook tabs represent priorities so that when you open your binder you will be reminded of what you have chosen to focus on in the order of their importance to you. This helps most people keep from getting overwhelmed. Place the tabs in the order of your priorities with the most urgent ones in the front of your workbook. They can be moved at any time as your priorities shift.

After achieving any goal, acknowledge how great it feels to have this part of your life working well and celebrate! Then write a celebration page and place it in the front to remind you. If this topic feels complete for now, move that tab and section of pages to the back. Be sure to keep only the pages that are clear and essential. You can re-name a tab for a new priority with a stick-on-label cut to size.

The following are powerful positive thoughts for each workbook topic. In your own handwriting, write the affirmation at the top of the first page in that section.

Health

What I do now for my body brings me health and pleasure.

Work

The work I have now becomes the work that I want.

Love

My needs for connection, friendship and intimacy are met.

Money

All the money I need comes to me now as I celebrate my true worth.

Fun

My life now becomes tons of fun in healthy ways.

Preparing to write

Your writing can, of course, happen anytime you feel moved to write. Take time out in a special place where you feel nurtured. Give yourself the luxury of writing regularly with a bit of quiet time before putting pen to paper. Use lined paper, or use pencil if writing on your workbook pages.

Find a quiet place in your environment or if this is not possible then take some time to find a place of quiet within. It may help to imagine being in a place that is beautiful and peaceful to you. Whenever possible sit with your most comfortable centered posture, and breathe slowly until you are relaxed before you begin to write. In the beginning just write whatever comes to mind after reading the section you are most attracted to. However you choose to begin, be patient with yourself because this can take a bit of practice. Soon it will be a habit and very easy for you.

When you are centered and relaxed it is possible to let go of the grip of mind and thought for awhile. Then you may notice the slower and wiser thoughts that arise from your center. If this sounds a bit strange right now, just give it a try and see what happens. Practice is not always necessary, sometimes letting go can be easy, so be open to this possibility.

"Things should be made as simple as possible, but not simpler." Einstein

Inspiring Yourself

Write these positive statements or any others you create for yourself on bright pieces of paper or index cards. Place them around your house, in your car, in your workspace, your purse or anywhere you will notice and read them.

I get the best possible help with my goals.

I accomplish my goals easily, creatively and actively.

I think positive and powerful thoughts and energetic actions naturally follow.

My goal is healthy and positive so it's therefore supported by life.

I do something big or small towards my goal each day.

The successful steps to my goal become clear after I begin.

I happily try new things and see which ones work for me.

I go after my needs and wants in positive healthy ways.

I find excellent ways to use my many abilities.

Desires as Goals

To create goals for ourselves we need to think that we have a chance to have some of the things we want. Without hope of success we would not have ideas for improvements or let ourselves desire anything better. This could mean a life without meaning or motivation. We can move out of such a state by practicing new thoughts and creating new feelings.

Change starts with the very first thought that "maybe we can achieve our goals and learn to feel great about ourselves." As soon as this kind of thinking begins, personal transformation can move quickly. With the energy generated by positive expectations, both inner, and outer changes begin to happen. Then we begin to move with the flow of life toward our blessings.

One simple way to move forward is to make every healthy desire into a goal by writing and thinking positive thoughts. Write statements saying that the goal is accomplished. At first this may not make sense and may be difficult to believe. For example, "The car I want is in my driveway and the keys are in my pocket." "I own it now." Proceeding in this way will help you practice having new expectations for what will happen in your life and what you will receive by putting yourself into the feeling state of the wish fulfilled. Even if you experience this feeling for just a few minutes a day it can move your life to a new level of creating what you desire.

Write these or any other affirmations you can think of in your own hand and style.

I now allow myself to have a better job with more income, enjoyment and benefits.

I am now doing the job I dream of and receiving what I need and want from it as I contribute my skills and energy happily.

I get to enjoy the job I dream of, working ____ hours per week while making $_____ per month.

I have complete quiet (or my favorite music) and my own work space.

I get to learn about my favorite topic _____ while I contribute _____ to others.

I get to have fun with others at work doing activities I really like.

I receive acknowledgement and appreciation as well as great pay for all my time.

I am enjoying many new and beautiful experiences beyond my previous dreams through all the great connections I make at my job.

You can write many pages like this on any topic that interests you.

Put your new pages away for a few days, then read and re-write them even more clearly and simply until they become a part of you. Be sure to write them in the present tense. Take the time you need to imagine and feel yourself in the state you will be in when the desires are fulfilled.

To get started, fill in the blanks below. Or repeat all the writing in your own personal way on a blank lined page in freehand.

I get to have...

_____

_____

_____

_____

_____

I am now finding a way to...

_____

_____

_____

_____

_____

My needs are being met in ways that are unknown to me at present, beginning with my need for...

_____

_____

_____

_____

_____

_____

_____

Each day I am grateful for the resources I have. This attracts more support and opportunities to me. Today I am grateful for...

_____

_____

_____

_____

_____

_____

_____

Fulfill Your Fantasies

If you have any unfulfilled longing or childhood fantasy about anything you want to do in this lifetime, a great way to get started with your writing process is to reclaim and explore them in your writing. Since I began this way of writing I have completed the following childhood and teen fantasies for myself. It has been a thrill and a great boost to my confidence.

Use this list as an example and make your own. Notice the "I get to" form of the statements. Practicing this kind of thinking can be a big boost to your level of hope and what you are able to manifest.

I get to...

Sing and dance on stage in front of an audience

Learn to scuba dive

Show my artwork in a one-woman exhibit

Write a book and publish it

Perform an autobiographical monologue

When you write your fantasy pages remember to aim for some dreams that are beyond your usual patterns of thinking. It's important to learn that we can achieve our goals without first knowing how. In this method, we begin without being able to imagine how it might happen.

We need a clear intention and an attitude that says "maybe anything is possible, even if I don't know how to make the change right now. Intend that your efforts will be successful and say it is so. This is called affirming.

Write in this type of affirmation and try to fill a whole page.

I get to have success beyond my previous ideas.

I am amazed to find the opportunities I have wanted for so long is here in my life this week, or this month, or this year.

All the support I need arrives.

I am now enjoying my job and all the people I work with.

I have all the friends and companions I can find time for.

I enjoy a great leap in my health and well being.

Learn to go wild when you write these and let yourself feel excited about your dreams.

The more you cultivate these thoughts and feelings the more abundance and satisfaction you will inevitably experience. You now have the opportunity like never before to achieve your goals for contributing to others through your work, business success, volunteerism and devotion to those close to you.

This process is powerful and will change your life if you take the time to write often and keep going. You will find out for yourself by your own results whether it is worthwhile. I am betting you will be amazed by the changes you can make in a short time. In the beginning I am going to tell you what to think, Just as my coach did with me. Later you will form a habit of positive inspired thinking on your own. To get started, think this or some similar thought as many times a day as possible, "Everything in life wants to move in a creative and prosperous direction so I can align myself with this natural movement and be provided with every need now."

During your day write down any troublesome feeling or negative thought, set it aside and go on with your day. This is a valuable practice because these thoughts become the raw material you need to create a goal. Later, write each of the thoughts again, changing it to a positive affirmation which will be literally the opposite. You must read and write it again, until you can imagine and believe it. Training yourself to think inspired new thoughts is an important part of self coaching.

Combine Affirmations with Actions

By writing affirmations you are beginning to cultivate the practice of transforming problems into goals and positive thoughts. The next key is using affirmations followed by action steps. You don't have to know what the actions will be at first, just write down any action steps you can think of after writing the affirmation. Stay open to more ideas coming later as you hold the goal in mind throughout your day. Write these ideas down right away while they are fresh in your mind. Write your action steps in a list below your affirmation. Be bold and try any ideas that might help you get to the goal. Here is one example of an affirmation followed by action steps...

My current project is going forward with the best possible help and ease. It is completed in one month and is very successful. I get a raise in my income and some new friends while having fun doing this project.

I research my goal on the web or library this week.

I call a few people who do something similar this week.

I purchase the materials to make my sample this week.

I go to work with my friend to see what he does there.

Transform Discouraging Thoughts

If we feel sad, angry or disappointed we can take responsibility to transform these feelings as soon as possible. Do this by writing and re-writing the thoughts that evoke them. This is an important part of what is meant by "writing our way through life." In addition to manifesting changes in our lives in troubling areas we also get a chance to let go of upset with ourselves and others.

It is wonderful to discover that we can change difficult feelings by using transformative writing and by practicing positive thoughts. So, if you're upset just write a complaints page. Then write a translation using the instructions below to begin changes.

Some people who begin this process will discover internal voices that can be discouraging, critical and judgmental. Please visualize a place where these feelings and ideas can be held in a locked safe or cave or a hole where they can be buried under a heavy lid or big rock.

In your imagination send these dark forces to a strong container where the cannot harm anyone. If you need help at this point you may want to share your writing with a Psychologist or other therapist of your choice.

Remember that having mean or negative thoughts does not mean you are bad. It is just a layer of your experience from the past. Whatever we have lost or never had in the past can be an major focus for transformation. For example, someone who moved often in childhood may want to focus on goals that support longevity of friendships or stability of home.

The process of writing through and transforming a past challenging experience will look something like this. Be sure to write in the past tense.

I had no dental care and my teeth fell apart.

It was painful and I was mad.

Make sure this is complete, including all of your feelings about the experience. Then write your healing affirmation in the present tense.

I now find ways to get all my dental care needs met.

And finally, write in the future tense.

I easily let go of any remaining emotions about my teeth.

I continue to have excellent dental care and I continue thinking positive thoughts about my dental health.

When negative thinking and feelings are revealed it is important to refrain from judging ourselves. We can make a safe place for the difficulty on the pages and transform them gradually.

We certainly can build a new mental and emotional habit by cultivating new thoughts and actions. Just write and re-write whatever message is showing up. Just as an alchemist changes coal into gold in the fairytales and legends of old, we have the power to transform a difficulty into a striength and use it for healing and transformation. We can make the worst things that have happened in our lives into conscious lessons, gifts of wisdom like fine medicine to offer ourselves and others. This happens when we reverse any negative thought by examining it and our feelings that arise, writing them all down, re-writing the main ideas as the exact opposite.

First, acknowledge any challenging thoughts, invite them to arise and be revealed but not believed. We can safely write and re-write these as new ideas, as positive healing thoughts. Then destroy the old pages with all the negative messages. Next, go back and focus on the positive ones. Keep doing this until the positive thoughts and feelings are strong. We can master our state of mind and feelings by writing often and by reading our own most positive writing.

After you have written the negative and the reverse of it, make a "new feelings" list and as you read it watch your emotions shift. Re-set and refresh yourself by simply reading the example list below. Notice how reading it makes you feel. Take some time to let each positive feeling settle into your body and mind. If any feelings on the list seem a challenge for now, simply come back to them later. Keep reading slowly to the bottom of the page. Read aloud if it is helpful or silently to yourself.

I am...

valuable

capable

supported

inspired

playful

authentic

confident

attractive

smart

worthy

"We have the power, just as the alchemists who changed coal into gold in the fairytales and legends of old. We can use it for our healing and transformation."

Notice Embedded Messages

Negative statements can sometimes creep into our writing in the form of what I call "embedded messages". An embedded message is one that is contained within another statement. It can take some concentration to notice an embedded message at first because it is hidden within the complete sentence. Here is an example of a seemingly positive statement that contains an embedded message:

"We each transform whatever problems arise in our relationship"

When you read this statement notice the embedded message "problems arise in our relationship." This is not something you would benefit from reading repeatedly. Notice any embedded messages and rewrite them.

Here is an example based on my experience. "I have many great friends, but I wonder why they don't call me." Do you see the embedded message? It is "they don't call me."

The most powerful re-write I can think of would be...

"I call my many friends often and they call me too. We love talking to each other."

Always look for a way the statement could be written more powerfully, positively and clearly. Keep it as simple as possible without leaving out anything truly important. Tear out and re-write anything that is less than inspiring to you. If you write anything complicated or confusing just tear it out and simplify it for your own clarity.

Eventually you will start to notice any time you speak an embedded message. Then the challenge, (and the opportunity), is to change the way you speak to make it more conscious and deliberate. When you get to this point, be sure to congratulate yourself because you are succeeding beautifully.

"A key factor is to have the experience of achieving a goal at least once and learn that we can achieve our goals without first knowing how. We begin without being able to imagine how it could happen."

Build Your Self Esteem

When we begin to succeed we may resist the new experience of feeling good about ourselves. This can come from old shame or early training that it was wrong to make positive statements about your self. It is essential to allow the new thoughts and feelings of self love and self worth so that you can keep writing affirmations and moving forward with your goals. It will help to write many celebration pages acknowledging your self and giving yourself praise. This is not only alright but it is essential for your mental and emotional well being.

When anything is challenging for you take some time to read all the supportive thoughts in your binder. They are affirmations of your value and qualities. You have plenty of them. At this challenging time you just need help to remember them. When you try something new, complete a step or accomplish anything, physically pat yourself on the back and say "Good job!" "You're awesome!" "Way to go!" Or, use some other words of praise that work for you.

"When you get to this point, be sure to congratulate yourself because you are succeeding beautifully."

Keep the Process Simple

As you move through the life making the changes you desire by writing your way, remember to keep only the positive pages and the most current and helpful. Toss the rest. Keep your binder in order and use only five tabs at a time with just five topics. If you ever feel scattered or overwhelmed, just restart yourself by cleaning out your binder and rewriting the most cluttered sections more clearly and simply.

Always tear out and re-write anything that is less than inspiring to you or anything complicated or confusing. Before ending a writing session, simplify your writing down to a few power point ideas to help you focus. If you ever feel overwhelmed, take out any complex pages and rewrite them in a much more simple form. You can save the complex ones in the back if you wish but remember to clear out any old inactive pages at least once a year.

Before closing your workbook make an effort to condense your most recent ideas or needs into a few very powerful thoughts. For example, If I write more and worry less I accomplish more, make more money, become more effective and get a needed rest. I always return to my writing and it supports my best life.

Balance with Self Care

I think it is a great thing to contribute to the needs of others as well as to ourselves. However contribution and work must be balanced by rest, enjoyment of life and self care or the result would be burn-out, which is an emotionally and physically exhausted state.

One way to know if you're taking good care of yourself is to ask if the path you are currently taking is truly rewarding. Are you receiving quality rewards for the efforts you put out for others in your work and life? Take some time to write about the rewards you receive from others and your appreciation of these rewards.

Spend some time noting the situations that do not reward you currently in ways that are important. Imagine a positive experience you can begin giving yourself. Maybe you could use some public or private acknowledgement for your qualities and contributions. Ask for rewards you want from your client, partner, lover, employer, co-workers, family or friends or give them to yourself.

Be bold and just a little "selfish" as you write a list of rewards you would like to receive. Maybe you have not had a vacation or healthy active fun in quite awhile. Imagine yourself with that need met, or stop everything that seems important, and spend an hour dancing or singing.

Be specific when you write about this topic. Here are a some examples.

I want to be seen and known for all those times I gave so many things in secret, or for what I did that seemed to be ignored or taken for granted.

Then, write some specific examples of these times:

Grandma does not know that I made all those dresses for her myself.

Dad didn't notice that I hauled his gift all the way from the top of the mountain.

No one acknowledged that I did all the cooking and clean up by myself. Next time I do all the dishes I will say, "Hey people, how about some applause and a foot massage."

Maybe it means asking someone to listen and to just say thank you. Or it could mean being compensated for something that was forgotten or that a promise needs to finally be kept. Whatever it is, make sure you get rewarded for your time and energy in some way if you want it, even if you have to negotiate for this.

It may mean a job change or a raise. For example, asking for it.

"I want to be paid for all my hours from now on and not just a flat salary. That means I get more per day for those long days."

Find ways you can reward yourself every step along the way or at the halfway mark of a goal or project. Then make sure you keep your promise to yourself, for example...

When I finish the first ten pages of my book I get to take a day off and go for a hike with a friend.

When I finish the first five chapters I will take a holiday somewhere I love to visit.

We can sometimes be a more reliable source of rewards for ourselves than others prove to be. This can get lonely if taken too far so be sure to seek out new friends who will celebrate with you, especially when you ask.

"If I write more and worry less I accomplish more, make more money, become more effective and get a needed rest. I always return to my writing and it supports my best life."

Gratitude and Celebration

I used to have a fear of becoming proud, seeming boastful or arrogant. I didn't know that feeling good about myself and my accomplishments was an important and healthy quality. As I became more successful in achieving goals I discovered that staying in a state of gratitude can be a remedy for excessive pride but that healthy pride is a good thing.

We can practice noticing what is supportive and generous in life, such as a quiet place to write or a comfortable chair. This can keep us humble and appreciative, in touch with the flow of abundance and receptive to more of life's gifts.

Try writing about your gratitude in a few different styles in the front section of your binder and continue to update it often. Practice speaking and writing your gratitude until this becomes a habit for you. Then make sure to go back and read these statements whenever you need a reminder of the greatness in your life. Focusing on these thoughts will help multiply them and the great possibilities of more to come.

"We can practice noticing what is supportive and generous in life, such as a true friend, a quiet place to write or a comfortable chair."

Here is my current gratitude list. The topic for this list is my completed workbook. Reading it is always a boost to my mood and self esteem.

I wish to express many thanks for help, love and support to...

My deceased coach Bob Loy, who would applaud this workbook and see a bit of himself in it.

My daughter, Kelly McGeehe, and granddaughter Christine Jones, for their hours of typing.

Abby Wasserman and Rana Di Orio-LeClaire for their indispensible editing

Jo Anne Smith for her design support positive spirit and patience

My dear friend John Orlando, for so many first experiences of the great things in life.

The infamous Noel Murphy, creator of "The Relationship Game" and "King Lessons" and "buckminster fuller Live" for being such a good friend to me from his heart.

And, to everyone who has told me that I have talent, ability and gifts to give. Although I enjoy independence in my creativity, I definitely value and need the caring and support from all of you.

Find a moment every day, maybe before you sleep, to celebrate something you accomplished. Develop the habit of writing a list of every little and big accomplishment you have created for yourself each week, or at least monthly. At the end of each year write celebration pages for each of the categories in your workbook. Here's one example.

Last month I...

Edited my book

Gave myself a $5 raise

Wrote letters to support the environment

Learned how to give myself a facial

Wrote letters and made phone calls to friends

Went to hear live music and see original art

Ate less fat and more salads

Took my vitamins regularly

Organized my closet and drawers

Keep your celebration pages at the front of your workbook where you will see and read them often. In every way you can think of, continue encouraging and praising yourself.

Review Your Goals

Write every small or major goal that you have ever achieved in your life time. When attempting to remember what you have done ask for help if you feel stuck. Be sure to ask someone who will promise to only tell you positive things. All of your accomplishments, from the smallest to the most grand are important. Use three pages minimum then read it and put it away where you will notice and re-read it at least annually. Write a new goals review each month and save it with your celebration pages.

Just before the end of each year review all of your goals and create a significant celebration. It could be alone in secret, with one trusted friend or in a group. Maybe it will be with close friends or family. However you choose to celebrate, make sure you do. Give yourself a reward and write plenty of celebration statements about your accomplishments for the year. Clear your binder of excess, keeping only the most positive and concise writing. Then write some new goals for the coming year that inspire you.

"Whatever you think you can do or believe you can do, begin it. Action has magic, grace and power in it." Johann Wolfgang von Goethe

Process Checklist

- ❧ Before you write, center your body, breathing slowly until you relax.

- ❧ Write goals as positive statements as if they are happening now.

- ❧ Make both fantastic and realistic goals.

- ❧ Imagine your goals are happening now.

- ❧ Make a list of actions to try out.

- ❧ Include a few out-of-the-ordinary ideas for your actions list.

- ❧ Try them and continue the ones that work.

- ❧ Read your writing often.

- ❧ Rewrite it more clearly as needed.

- ❧ Celebrate and write accomplishments and gratitude lists.

- ❧ Continue to clarify, organize and prioritize goals.

- ❧ Clear out your workbook often, removing all clutter.

- ❧ Review your accomplishments and write new goals annually.

"Build your self esteem and sense of worth and learn to practice self-care. Help, opportunities and all the support you need will follow."

Start a Support Group

The copyright for *Writing our Way Through Life, A Self-Coaching Workbook* is owned by the author, Christie Close of Marin County, California.

If any school, organization, individual, therapist or teacher wants to use all or any portion of this manuscript to teach classes or workshops I would like to be contacted and asked for permission. I am generous about sharing the pages but would like to know where it is being used and with what population.

If this workbook is used in a goals support group I suggest that participants read, share and celebrate every big and little accomplishment and avoid the temptation to evaluate anyone's progress. Each person writes as they are moved and progresses at their own pace. I believe groups that allow only congratulations are the most helpful. They provide a safe place where no one evaluates you but yourself. You validate all of your own process and no one judges the goals you choose or your actions toward your dreams. To start a Marin or San Francisco support group please contact *christie@newparentcoaching.com*.

48856692R00020

Made in the USA
San Bernardino, CA
19 August 2019